Donna Brandes

Cartoons by Fanny Tribble

GAMESTERS'
HANDBOOK TWO

Another collection of games for teachers and group workers
by the co-author of **Gamesters' Handbook**

Stanley Thornes (Publishers) Ltd

First published in ring-binder by Access Publishing, Leeds, 1982
This edition first published by Hutchinson Education 1984

Reprinted 1990 by
Stanley Thornes (Publishers) Ltd
Ellenborough House
Wellington Street
CHELTENHAM GL50 1YW
England

97 98 99 00 / 20 19 18 17 16 15 14 13 12

ISBN 0 7487 0322 5
Photoset in Univers

By the same author

Gamesters' Handbook (with Howard Phillips): Stanley Thornes;

The Hope Street Experience: Access Printing, Leeds (1981)

Printed and bound in Great Britain
by Redwood Books, Trowbridge, Wiltshire

CONTENTS

Introduction   7
All purpose games   13
Introductory games   93
Group leaders' games   123
Conclusion   137

DEDICATION: TO DIANE HOWARD

This book is lovingly dedicated to my friend, Diane Howard, because without her support, encouragement and friendship I might not have completed it. Diane also contributed at least two dozen of the games and helped clarify many others. Her strength and humour and aliveness have been an inspiration to me.

ACKNOWLEDGEMENTS

To Martin Evans, for his outrageous humour and his help in making this publication possible.

To Howard Baker for being 'an author's publisher'.

To Sandie Buckell for her support, excellent ideas and intensive typing at the last minute.

To Steve Myers, who was with me when we first began to use games, years ago.

To Howard Phillips with whom I collaborated on **Gamesters' Handbook** for his sharing, his humour and his love of games.

To Tom Adams for his invention, fun and creativity.

To Walter Truman-Cox for inventing Funogetics and for his playfulness.

To Cindy Howard for faithfully collecting and writing down the games as they were invented.

To Nick Kell, my former partner, for inventing a lot of these games when we used to work together.

To Chris White for his exuberance and gamesmanship.

To Penny Minney for knowing hundreds of quaint and unusual games.

To Dorothy Heathcote, Werner Erhard and Carl Rogers – my heroes.

To anyone I absent-mindedly forgot to acknowledge here ....

And to all the people, in hundreds of courses over the past five years who were told to 'Go away and invent a game for ....' and who went away and did it. Here they are and I thank you for your creations. These games are for all of us to use and share with each other.

FIVE YEARS OF GAMESTERSHIP

In the past five years since the publication of **Gamesters' Handbook**, it has been very exciting to watch its growth as orders have come in from all over the world. In the UK, America, New Zealand, France and Australia, the book has been ordered by teachers, group leaders, youth workers, social workers, clergy, families, voluntary organisations, nurses, doctors, psychiatrists, yoga teachers, health visitors, health education officers, boy scouts, girl guides, prison officers, probation officers and many more.

As I've travelled around running groups and courses in England and America, certain games have turned out to be my favourites because they are versatile, require no planning or materials, and because they always work ... that is, they tend **not** to go wrong. These include: **Rule of the Game, Sabotage, Adverb Game, American Charades, Indian Tepee, Value Continuum, How do you like your neighbour, Merry-go-round, Human Noughts and Crosses, Toyshop, The Waiting Game, Tick Tock, Alice in Wonderland, Bumpety-Bump-Bump,** and above all **Brainstorming. Brainstorming** involves the whole group in a non-threatening way, and, as all answers are accepted without comment, it has the effect that people feel their contributions are valued, thus beginning to provide a comfortable climate for learning. **Brainstorming** is not really a game; it is a way of teaching and a way of life. As I learnt for myself and from reading Carl Rogers, I know I can't teach anyone anything, I can only provide a climate in which people can learn.

FRIENDLY COMMENT TO GAMESTERS

These games are not meant to be played only at the end of a lesson or a group when there is a bit of time left over, although they are useful that way. They are meant to be: (1) expanded, (2) shared and developed, (3) adapted and applied to all areas of any curriculum, (4) internalised so that you can throw the book away, (5) carefully evaluated as to their enjoyment and learning value to your players.

Donna Brandes, 1982

INTRODUCTION

I am a games freak, a life-long addict. Games are not just an enjoyment to me, more a way of life. I play them with my friends, with teachers, social workers and small children; at parties, on trains, in groups, in school. **Gamester's Handbook** is partly a collection that I made while I was teaching. In 1977 I combined my collection with that of Howard Phillips, also a teacher, to produce the handbook which has brought me in contact with gamesters all over the world.

Games can be used constructively and not as pointless activities. Each game can have a different purpose which can always be defined – even fun is purposeful. Games can help sort out problems, the kinds of problems found in inter-personal relationships. They can help social inadequacy by developing co-operation within groups, develop sensitivity to the problems of others through games needing trust, and promote interdependency and a sense of personal identity.

Games can also enable the promotion of effective communication. Their usefulness in this direction cannot be overemphasised. By helping people to relax in groups, games can promote the flow of communication between complete strangers – particularly important with shy people who need additional encouragement.

The 'role playing' aspects of many games provide the security which enables group members to develop their ideas and express themselves. The enjoyment which can be generated by games does more than anything to develop a group identity. This fun can act as the basic ingredient for any group, and can develop cohesion and an open, accepting atmosphere more readily than anything else.

Sitting in a circle, rather than in rows of chairs or in a random setting, can influence group dynamics. It gives the same status to everyone, including the leader, and allows a much greater degree of eye contact. Within the circle people should be able to voice their opinions or feelings without the risk of being judged or laughed at. It is up to the leader of the group to ensure that this freedom is understood and respected.

A 'round' is the process by which each person, progressing the circle in turn, makes a statement completing one of the following: I noticed ... (particularly good for films etc.); I discovered ... (especially after a new experience or game); I wish ...; I learned ...; I resent ...; I appreciate ... The latter two are highly recommended for evaluating an experience. One round of 'I resent' followed by one round of 'I appreciate' enables everyone to express both negative and positive feelings in that order.

When doing rounds, everyone must listen quietly to the person speaking, and no comments are to be made, even by the leader. If a statement is made which necessitates discussion, this should be saved until after the rounds are completed. Anyone can refuse a turn by saying 'I pass' and there should be no comment about this either. This structure can be used for many purposes, including discussing and evaluating anything from a film or a game to a personal experience; planning group meetings; problem solving and positive reinforcement.

Waiting Game can remove much of the need for maintaining discipline on the part of the leader. Tell the group that you are not going to fight for their attention or quiet, that whenever they are together as a group for instruction or discussion, you will just wait until they are ready to listen. Tell them that it is called **Waiting Game** and that you will not take the responsibility for getting their attention, that they must take it themselves.

The leader's waiting must have a quality of nothingness – no resignation or martyred patience – all questions and interruptions must be ignored. It must also be a non-threatening attitude; don't worry about the time you are wasting. If you persevere with them in the beginning, you will save great quantities of time and effort later.

Remember, the idea behind the waiting game is that the members of the group take responsibility for how they are behaving, not the group leader. If they use group time at first to chat with each other, they will soon get bored and express a preference for active happenings. You must be patient and consistent and play it every time or it will not work.

Whatever problems or concerns you are having with any given group are not your problems, they are the group's problems, so don't try to solve them at home when lying in bed at night. Tell the problem to the group and ask for ideas and feelings about it. Remember, you are as much a member of the group as anyone else; you should share your feelings and problems with them if you want real group interaction.

The leader has to have certain basic attitudes in order to use the games effectively. If these attitudes are not authentic, or only superficial, the others in the group will be able to sense the pretence. In fact, it would be ideal if prospective leaders and users of **Gamesters' Handbook** had to pass an attitude test. Try it for yourself: just read the following questions and answer them in your head – honestly. (Who do you think you're kidding anyway?)

8

Merging with the group:

* Are you willing to give up the hierarchy and stop being the authority figure who has all the answers?
* Are you willing to hand over responsibility to the individuals in the group?
* Are you willing to truly accept any answer that comes from the group?
* Are you willing to be there as a facilitator and give control to each person in the group?
* Do you really believe that everyone is capable of taking responsibility for him or her self?

Losing your investment in how things go:

* Can you stand the uncertainty of not knowing how any game and situation might turn out?
* Can you adopt a fail-safe attitude that says, 'there is no way things can go wrong because whatever happens I can help the group to learn from it'?
* Can you give up always being right about everything?

Accepting others:

* Can you accept that your way of thinking/believing may not fit everybody?
* Can you refrain from imposing your views on others?
* Do you react negatively to anyone who looks, acts, speaks, dresses, behaves, thinks, values things differently from the way you think they should? (Come on, **everybody** has to say 'yes' to that one if they're being honest.)

Having a sense of humour:

* Will your sense of humour stretch to letting you see the funny side of any situation you get into?

How did you do on the test? That's OK! I really believe that you can train yourself to be a facilitating, accepting, non-judging, fun-loving leader.

WAIT A MINUTE, DON'T PANIC. . . I'm not talking about being 'permissive' (horrible word). In fact that's incongruous because you also have to give up the idea of permission.

The standards set for a group like this are very strict and I as leader have to be assertive about working towards them. I have to know what I want and make it very clear. We are going to listen to each other and value each other's contribution, even though we may not agree. We are going to learn from each other. Each of us is 100% responsible for how this group goes. Each of us can make this group into a learning experience – or sabotage that effort.

Again, I am not talking about being 'permissive' but the above goals are reached by being very patient and acknowledging positive behaviour. Being willing to remind people over and over again of what we are trying to accomplish. Any hint of punishment or personal rejection will take me away from the goal of self-responsibility for each member of the group. When a trace of authoritarianism creeps in, it is difficult to get back to the cohesiveness we were trying to build.

I could write a separate book on how trust develops in a group – it's a by-product of all the attitudes mentioned above. I can only evoke trust by being trustworthy. If I don't mean what I say, keep my agreements, communicate what I'm doing and intending to do, then my leadership turns into manipulation. If I don't absolutely trust the people I'm working with (or at the very least communicate about and clear up my mistrust), how can I expect anyone else to trust me?

Let's take one specific game from **Gamesters' Handbook** and follow it through:

RULE OF THE GAME

Materials None.

Aims Group interaction, imagination, intellectual exercise, fun, getting to know each other.

Procedure Form a circle. One person goes out and the others choose a rule. When that person returns he or she must find out the rule by asking people questions about themselves. A good rule to begin with is to answer every question as if you were the person on your right. Players must answer questions honestly, according to the rules. Another possibility would be for all girls to tell lies and all men to tell the truth.

Rules can be very hard or very simple, according to age and experience. Rules can be visual (scratch your head before answering), or structural

10

(each answer to begin with the next letter of the alphabet).

Anyone who doesn't feel like joining in is free to say nothing or 'I pass'. The only way to get everyone to participate is to allow everyone **not** to participate. This applies to all the games; everyone is invited to join in, no one is excluded and no one is chastised for staying out. I have always found that if children are free not to participate, then eventually they will want to.

In **Rule of the game** as in **Crossed and uncrossed** and **Adverb game** and others of this genre, everyone knows something except the one who has gone out of the room. If the leader is effective then the game will develop such that everyone is supporting the person who is 'it', not keeping him or her guessing as long as possible. One of the primary aims of this game is group co-operation – while one person has been temporarily excluded from the group, that person will soon be 'in' and someone else will be 'out'.

I have expressed a lot of positive ideas about using games in groups, most of which result from my experience as a teacher, therapist and group leader. However, I must acknowledge that youth clubs and community centres, as settings, provide special problems for using the games.

The purpose-built centres which became popular in the seventies are designed by authorities who want large numbers of people to attend them. They are ideal for sport and large group activities (discos etc.) but there is rarely a place where a small group can meet without interruption. The public rooms are generally too big – all glass and high ceilings – which does not promote communication. Committee rooms are usually reserved for the management team, and are rarely available for young people to use for meetings or quiet places where they could talk or do homework. Furthermore, the young people would not be accustomed to the group-work format or goals in the youth club setting. A youth or community worker would have to put considerable energy into gathering an interested group and gaining their confidence.

I know many youth and community workers who use games to good purpose, and who find them extremely useful in establishing contact and communication with their clients. They persist with the management committee until they are given a place to meet. They learn to change their own attitudes so that the games are used productively, and they encourage an initially small group to welcome new members and absorb them into the group.

Donna Brandes, 1982

This introduction was written with the support and assistance of Nick Kell,

Dave Hull and Madeleine Knight and was first published in Youth and Society in April 1980 under the title **The Confessions of a Games Freak.**

ALL-PURPOSE GAMES

CONTENTS

A.P.1.   What's happening ?   Page 19

A.P.2.   Spots   Page 20

A.P.3.   Song title game   Page 21

A.P.4.   Parent biographies   Page 22

A.P.5.   The birthday game   Page 23

A.P.6.   Botticelli   Page 24

A.P.7.   The interview game   Page 26

A.P.8.   Closing rounds   Page 27

A.P.9.   Marriage guidance   Page 28

A.P.10. Alice in wonderland   Page 29

A.P.11. The tortoise game   Page 30

A.P.12. Wave the ocean   Page 31

A.P.13. Instant mottoes   Page 32

A.P.14. Call my bluff   Page 33

A.P.15. Classic spin the bottle   Page 34

A.P.16. Spin the bottle (Mark II)   Page 36

A.P.17. English charades   Page 37

A.P.18. Rabbits and ferrets   Page 38

A.P.19. Witches   Page 39

A.P.20. Bears   Page 40

A.P.21. Assertiveness Game (1)   Page 41

A.P.22. Assertiveness Game (2)   Page 42

A.P.23. Assertiveness Game (3)   Page 44

A.P.24. Assertiveness Game (4)   Page 45

15

A.P.25. Invention   Page 47

A.P.26. On to the next world   Page 48

A.P.27. Electric chair   Page 50

A.P.28. Suddenly   Page 51

A.P.29. The pride line   Page 52

A.P.30. Joy of being   Page 53

A.P.31. People to people   Page 54

A.P.32. The time machine (fantasy)   Page 55

A.P.33. Put your money where your mouth is   Page 57

A.P.34. Attending – non-attending   Page 58

A.P.35. Time capsule   Page 59

A.P.36. Freud   Page 60

A.P.37. Feeling circle   Page 62

A.P.38. People rolling   Page 63

A.P.39. Murphy's law   Page 64

A.P.40. Sherlock Holmes (Mark II)   Page 65

A.P.41. Snake in the grass   Page 66

A.P.42. Value cards   Page 68

A.P.43. Blindman's numbers   Page 69

A.P.44. Knee tapping   Page 70

A.P.45. General post   Page 71

A.P.46. The old family coach   Page 72

A.P.47. Locomotion   Page 73

A.P.48. Who has the ball ?   Page 74

A.P.49. Department store   Page 75

A.P.50. Name six   Page 77

A.P.51. Name six (Mark II)   Page 78

A.P.52. Shoe carry race   Page 79

A.P.53. Liar   Page 80

A.P.54. Move to the spot   Page 81

A.P.55. Shoepile   Page 82

A.P.56. Shoe circle   Page 83

A.P.57. Shoelace relay   Page 84

A.P.58. Walter's toes   Page 85

A.P.59. Chequerboard   Page 86

A.P.60. Crossed and uncrossed   Page 88

A.P.61. Mister Men   Page 89

A.P.62. Tag variations   Page 90

WHAT'S HAPPENING ?

Materials: None.

Aims: Fun, drama warm-up, lateral thinking.

Procedure: One person goes out of the room. People in the room arrange themselves into a scene or situation. When the person returns he/she has to guess what is happening there, e.g. everyone is dying of the plague. He/she keeps asking questions until the situation is revealed.

Variations: Ask only 'yes' or 'no' questions. Mime the questions as in charades.

SPOTS

Materials: Large empty room or space.

Aims: Learning to follow simple instructions, movement, drama warm-up.

Procedure: Leader says, 'Find a place to stand by yourself. Now look at and concentrate on a fixed spot on the floor, somewhere across the room. Now, move to that spot in a straight line, pacing yourself so as not to have to stop, while avoiding bumping into anyone.'
Leader continues to give similar instructions, allowing time for individuals to (A) Concentrate on each spot, (B) Move at their own pace, and (C) Settle into the new spot.
Some instructions might be: Move to the new spot:
1. Backwards.
2. In as few stops as possible.
3. In as many steps as possible.
4. Travelling in circles.
5. Travelling in squares.
6. Using as few jumps as possible.
7. With hands on knees, toes etc.
8. Moving along floor without using hands etc.
9. With a partner, using only two out of four legs.
10. Reflecting various emotions, e.g. fear etc.

Variations: Have group invent more instructions.

SONG TITLE GAME

Materials: None.

Aims: Fun, lateral thinking, amusement while travelling, communication.

Procedure: Think of a song title, e.g. **I'm singing in the rain.** Make up rhyming words for the title e.g. I'm bringing in the cane. Now make up a riddle or story to go with it, e.g. What did the farmer say when he was harvesting the sugar crop ? Now tell the other players the riddle and wait for them to guess the title.

A.P.4.

PARENT BIOGRAPHIES

Materials: None.

Aims: Self-disclosure, memory, self-awareness, exploring parental relationships.

Procedure: Sit quietly with your eyes shut and think about your parents. Think of the parent about whose life you know the most. Remember as many things about that parent as you can. Become that parent. Look around the room and pick a partner that you want to work with. When you have a partner decide which one is A and which is B. A tells B about his/her parent as if he/she were that parent. B listens then does the same. Then the partners take turns to tell each other about the parent now and in the future, still being that parent. The amount of time allowed for these interchanges can be flexible-probably three to five minutes. Return to the circle and do a round in which people say what feelings came up for them during this exercise.

THE BIRTHDAY GAME

Materials: Birthday cake and candles.

Aims: Personal development, sensitivity, celebration.

Procedure: Divide the number of years of your life by five. (Extra years can be counted as a separate group, e.g. a person of fifty three would have five sections of ten years and one of three).
Close your eyes and think about your life in general. Then think about life in the first section of years and share one memory of it with the people present. Continue this through the other sections. End with two wishes, one made out loud and one made silently.

Variations: Everyone at the birthday has a go. Play it at Christmas and other occasions when family and friends are gathered together.
With small children parents and friends can help by saying, 'Remember when . . .'

BOTTICELLI

Materials: None.

Aims: Imagination, lateral thinking, group inter-action, fun, historical awareness.

Procedure: Can be played by any number of people from two upwards. One member of the group thinks of a famous person and tells the group the initial letter of his/her surname. The group members then ask questions, e.g. 'Are you a famous actor?' 'Are you a famous author?' If the occupation guessed does not fit, the person answering must answer in the negative, giving an example of someone from that category whose surname starts with the same letter. The questioner must also be thinking of someone in that category with the same initial letter to their surname when he/she asks the question. Thus: if the example was Botticelli, then the answers to the above questions could be, 'No, I am not Humphrey Bogart.' 'No, I am not Francis Bacon.' If the answerer cannot think of someone famous in the same category with the same initial, and the questioner can, then the questioner may ask a direct question, e.g. 'Are you dead?' When the correct occupation is guessed the answerer may be elusive by thinking of someone else in the same category with the same initial letter: 'Yes, I am a painter but I am not William Blake.' The game goes on until the questioners guess the identity of the famous person.

Variations: It can be played the other way round with the whole group being the famous person and one person asking the questions.
Use friends as the 'famous people.'

THE INTERVIEW GAME

Materials: None.

Aims: Imagination, improvisation, lateral thinking, fun.

Procedure: One person goes out of the room and while the person is out the group chooses a job for which to interview him/her, e.g. Beefeater in the Tower of London. When they have decided, the person outside the room returns for an interview not knowing what job he/she is being interviewed for. The group then begins asking questions such as 'Do you mind wearing a uniform?' 'Do you like dressing up?' 'Are you fond of ravens?' 'Do you like to work near water?'. Each question must give hints but should not give the game away. The person being interviewed must answer the questions as though in an interview. When the group thinks the interviewee knows the answer they can offer him/her the job. The interviewee then replies, indicating that he/she knows the answer, 'Yes, I would like to be a beefeater', or 'No, I would not like to be a beefeater.' If the answer is wrong the group will probably have collapsed laughing.

A.P.8.

CLOSING ROUNDS

For evaluation and closure purposes do a round of:

What am I taking away with me from this group ?

What I'll think of on the way home and wish I had said or done.

The most boring/exciting part of this group for me was .....

Something I have discovered today .....

The homework I am giving myself for next week is ......

My new friend from this group is .....

MARRIAGE GUIDANCE

Materials: One cushion or pillow for each player.

Aims: To break down inhibitions, warm-up, fun, release energy.

Procedure: The participants line up in two teams and face each other. Each person has a pillow. The leader can either play or stand to one side. The leader explains that he/she is going to call out various numbers and that each number has an instruction attached:
ONE: Hit members of the other team with pillows.
TWO: Insult members of the other team.
THREE: Compliment members of the other team.
FOUR: Fall to the ground in a faint. The leader calls the numbers at random (and whim).

Variations: Reverse the numbers of one team so that the two teams are reacting differently to the same numbers.
Add more numbers and instructions.
Use nonsense words, nouns, letters instead of numbers.

ALICE IN WONDERLAND

Materials: None.

Aims: Imagination, lateral thinking, group interaction, fun, historical awareness.

Procedure: Can be played by any number of people from
two upwards. One person thinks of a famous
character, e.g. Alice in Wonderland. The other
person or people ask questions to discover the
identity of the famous character. The questions
are asked according to the following format:
Q: If I were a food, what food would I be ?
A: A mushroom or a piece of cake, (or anything
reminiscent of Alice in Wonderland).
Q: If I were an animal, what animal would I be ?
A: A dormouse or a white rabbit.
Categories of questions could include: songs,
musical instruments, birds, drinks, centuries,
modes of transport and anything else the
questioner can devise.

Variations: It can be played the other way round with the
whole group being a famous character and one
person asking the questions.
Use friends as the famous characters.

THE TORTOISE GAME

Materials: None.

Aims: Warm-up, fun, relaxation, trust-building.

Procedure: People sit around the outside wall of the room. They aim to cross the room diagonally on 'all fours'. Each person takes a number, 1, 2 or 3, and when that number is called they move one limb at a time until they have reached the other side of the room.

Variations: The game can be played with people lying on the floor and they can make one movement when their number has been called.

WAVE THE OCEAN

Materials: None.

Aims: Fun, warm-up.

Procedure: The group sit on chairs in a circle. Two chairs are empty. One person stands in the middle. When the leader says, 'Wave to the left', the whole group move left around the chairs, keeping their faces towards the middle of the circle and moving around in a sitting position. (If the leader says, 'Wave to the right', they move to the right.) The person in the middle tries to sit on a chair. when he/she succeeds, the person on his/her right moves to the centre, and, (after a short rest !) the game continues.

INSTANT MOTTOES

Materials: None.

Aims: Group interaction, imagination, decision-making.

Procedure: Each person makes up a motto which represents the experience the group has had together. Join a partner and take one minute to compromise on a motto. Join another pair, reach compromise and continue until the whole group makes a final motto.

CALL MY BLUFF

Materials: Dictionary, pens/pencils, paper.

Aims: Group interaction, fun, imagination.

Procedure: One person chooses a word from the dictionary and checks that no one in the group knows its meaning. Each other person in the group gets a piece of paper and writes down a definition and the papers are then placed in a pile. The person who chose the word then asks everyone to vote from the pile of definitions (one of which will be the correct definition).

Variations: The game can be played in teams.

CLASSIC SPIN THE BOTTLE

Materials: A bottle.

Aims: Touch, fun, ice-breaker.

Procedure: Someone spins the bottle and whoever it points at gets a kiss, a hug, or a compliment from the spinner.

Variations: Keep spinning the bottle until everyone has a partner. This can be used prior to games requiring 'pairs'.

"You're too beautiful to kiss"

SPIN THE BOTTLE (Mark II)

Materials: A bottle.

Aims: Self-disclosure, trust development, vocalising needs, self-validation, sharing, confidence, group cohesion.

Procedure: The group sits in circles of five to eight people with a bottle in the middle. One person can start by answering the question, 'What are my personal needs from this group?' They then spin the bottle and when it stops the person who is sitting opposite the neck of the bottle should answer the question and then spin the bottle again.

Variations: This could be repeated with people saying how the group could move towards meeting these needs.

ENGLISH CHARADES

Materials: Paper and pencils.

Aims: Group cohesion, fun imagination, creativity, drama skills.

Procedure: Work in small groups. The leader gives each group a piece of paper with a word on it, e.g. piety, despair. The group then designs a presentation to enact and the other groups have to guess what the particular word is.

Variations: Adverb game.

N.B. See also American Charades in **The Gamesters Handbook**. The purpose of English Charades is to confuse the other team. The purpose of American Charades (pronounced 'charaydes') is to be very clear and communicate ideas to your own team. This difference in intent may seem subtle to you but is crucial to true afficianados.

RABBITS AND FERRETS

Materials: None.

Aims: Listening skills, group interaction, sensitivity, fun.

Procedure: This game is played in a pitch dark room. Two members are ferrets, the rest are rabbits, and the room in which the game is played is the 'warren'. The ferrets leave the room while the remainder check that there are no chinks of light, re-arrange themselves and other obstacles if they wish, and hide themselves as high or low as they like. Then the lights are put out and the ferrets are called. They come, closing the door behind them and, by listening, they have to locate and catch the rabbits. Also by listening, the rabbits have to get past them without being caught and must touch the door.

WITCHES

Materials: None.

Aims: Group interaction, fun, guessing, pretending.

Procedure: The game needs to be played in a fairly dark room with space to run about. The players stand in a circle with their hands behind their backs. The leader goes round the outside and quietly touches one person's hand and that person becomes the witch. The leader tells the circle to scatter. As no one knows who is the witch members can chase each other, pretending to be the witch, but only the real witch can actually press a person's hand and add another witch to the number. This goes on until there is only one non-witch left.

Variations: Instead of touching, each person goes around and when they meet someone they say 'pruey, pruey' and the witch will be the one who doesn't respond. The aim is for everyone to find out who the witch is and, when she has been found, hold hands to form a chain.

BEARS

Materials: None.

Aims: Group interaction, fun, searching.

Procedure: This game will be best played in a house big enough to have two landings, or out of doors in woods or farm buildings. Two bears hide themselves, the hunters have to try and find them and the aim is to see one of the bears silhouetted, and then get back to base without being ambushed by the other bear.

ASSERTIVENESS GAME (1)

Materials: None.

Aims: Assertiveness training, role play, self-awareness, self-development.

Procedure:

(1) Brainstorm with the group definitions of the following types of behaviour: non-assertive, aggressive and assertive. What the leader is looking for is an actual description of how these people behave, their eye-contact, tone of voice etc. The leader should ask the question, 'If someone is going to lose or get hurt in a situation, who will it be?' (referring to each of the three descriptions, e.g. a non-assertive person is likely to get hurt or lose in any situation; an assertive person tries to set up a situation where no-one loses).

(2) In small groups of three or four, have people share the kinds of situations in which they themselves find it difficult to be assertive.

(3) The leader asks various groups to describe some of these situations.

(4) One situation is chosen for role play. For example:

Mrs. A. is returning something to a shop and wants her money back. Shopkeeper is to respond to Mrs. A. in the way that seems appropriate. Mrs. A. will first try the transaction in a non-assertive manner, then in an aggressive manner. The leader should coach Mrs. A. in finding an assertive way to deal with the matter, and Mrs. A. and the shopkeeper should find a way to compromise.

A.P.22

ASSERTIVENESS GAME (2)

Materials: None.

Aims: Assertiveness training, role play, self-awareness, self-development.

Procedure: Numbers (1) and (2) from **Assertiveness Game 1** should have been completed.

(3)   Divide the total group into groups of threes. In each group decide which is A, B, and C.

(4)   Have all the group members think of an idea they want to communicate to the other two members of the group, e.g. selling something to them, convincing them of something, criticising them for something etc.

(5)   In the first round, A is non-assertive, B is aggressive and C is assertive.

(6) A is the first to try to communicate. B and C respond according to the behaviour they have been assigned.

(7) If the game is played to its completion, each person gets a chance of playing each role of convincer and in each form of behaviour. (Nine rounds)

(8) Have each small group share their experience, describing how they felt in each role and telling the others which roles are most comfortable for them.

(9) Discuss in larger groups.

ASSERTIVENESS GAME (3)

Materials: None.

Aims: Assertiveness training, role play, self-aware-ness, self-development.

Procedure:

Numbers (1) and (2) from Game (1) should have been completed.

(3) Have everyone in the group close their eyes and imagine themselves in a forest. The leader should describe the forest in some detail making it sound as real as possible.

(4) The leader says, 'You are a very meek animal. You meet someone you know (in animal form) who is very aggressive. Imagine what happens when the two animals meet. Now switch roles – you are an aggressive animal and you meet someone who is much weaker. Finally, imagine yourself in the form of an animal you would really like to be. Imagine you meet someone you love, also in animal form. What happens when those animals meet?'

(5) a. Draw your forest scene and hang the pictures on the wall with bluetack, doing an 'Art Gallery Tour' of each picture.

OR

b. Have people take the roles of the different animals and act out the scene.

OR

c. Divide the whole group into three teams. One team represents the aggressive animals, one the meek animals and one the assertive or rescuing animals. (N.B. This is related to the T.A. concept of the Karpman Triangle, i.e. victim, persecutor and rescuer).

A.P.24

ASSERTIVENESS GAME (4)

Materials: None.

Aims: Assertiveness training, role play, self-awareness, self-development.

Procedure: There is no limit to the number of role play situations you can invent which explore the three types of behaviour described in the Assertiveness Games. Here are some examples we have thought of:

A train compartment with all three types in.

Three tribes each bearing one of the traits.

Prisoners, guards and liberating army.

Situations which explore racism, sexism and other social issues.

Confrontations at the gates of heaven/hell etc.

School situations.

Human obstacle course.

INVENTION

Materials: Paper, Pens or pencils.

Aims: Generating ideas, creative use of the imagination, group cohesion, fun, lateral thinking.

Procedure:

(1)   In large groups the leader asks the members to 'brainstorm' all subjects taught at school.

(2)   Divide into small groups of four or five and each group pick three specific subjects and 'brainstorm' the elements of each, e.g. craft, sewing, knitting, woodwork etc.

(3)   Each group then invents a game which includes all the elements of the chosen subject.

(4)   Present the game either by playing it group by group or asking the whole group to play the game.

ON TO THE NEXT WORLD

Materials: Paper, pens or pencils.

Aims: Self-awareness, creative writing, self-disclosure.

Procedure: (1)   Draw your tombstone and write the epitaph as you would like it to appear.
              (2)   Write the elegy that you would like to be said at your funeral.
              (3)   Design your funeral, including the music, setting, and guest list and your instructions for burial or whatever.

ELECTRIC CHAIR

Materials: One chair or, preferably, a large cushion.

Aims: Fun, physical activity.
(N.B. This game is for larger groups and can be rough.)

Procedure: Entire group links arms in a circle with the 'electric chair' in the centre. The object is to get people to touch the chair. Anyone who touches it is 'dead' and must leave the circle. Thus the circle keeps getting smaller.

Variations: Play game with eyes closed.
Backs to the centre.
Substitute a small group of people for the 'electric chair'.

SUDDENLY

Materials: None.

Aims: Creative thinking, ice-breaking, listening, reassuring, lateral thinking, choices.

Procedure: Everyone sits in a circle. Someone gives a sentence or short paragraph. When they stop, the person sitting next to them shouts 'Suddenly ....' and either adds something to it or uses the last word in it that could have two meanings and change the sense of the story. (e.g. 'Suddenly I saw a brown hair on his shoulder .....' 'Suddenly I realised that the little hare was hopping off across the field'). This is continued round the circle.

Variations: Give the group tickets with words on them that must be used.
Ask for a forfeit or fine for repeating certain words.

THE PRIDE LINE

Materials: None.

Aims: Positive self-concept, values clarification, self-disclosure.

Procedure: In rounds, the group members finish off the sentence, 'I'm proud that ...'

Some suggested items are:

Things you've done for your parents.
Things you've done for a friend.
Things you've done for yourself.
Things you've made.
How you spend your free time.
Habits you have.
Some things you tried hard for.
How you've earned some money.
Something you believe in.
A new skill you have acquired.
The nicest thing you did for someone last week.

Variations: Each person in the group has a turn to be the focus. Others in the group give the focal person positive feedback by saying, 'I'm .... and I'm proud that I have a good singing voice' etc.

JOY OF BEING

Materials: To be decided by the various groups.

Aims: Creative use of the imagination, group interaction, entertainment.

Procedure: Small groups. Each group chooses one of the following themes:

Joy of festivities.
Joy of fantasy.
Joy of creativity.
Joy of childhood.

It is then up to each particular group to decide how they will present their activity. They may decide to do it by themselves or to involve the whole group. e.g. 'Festivities' may decide to make a meal for everyone etc.

This game is generally played over three to four hours.

Variations: Each area and room in the house could be marked a specific 'joy' area, and the members are free to choose which rooms they go into as long as they participate in the activities in each room.

PEOPLE TO PEOPLE

Materials: None.

Aims: Warm-up, fun, group interaction.

Procedure: Players find a partner. The odd one out is the referee and calls out actions e.g. nose-to-nose, back-to-back, head-to-knee etc. When the referee calls 'People to people' everyone must change partners. The one who is left over becomes the new referee.

THE TIME MACHINE (FANTASY)

Materials: None.

Aims: Imagination, relaxation, self-awareness.

Procedure: The leader informs the group that he/she wants to lead them in a fantasy that has been dreamed about by writers for ages.

'I want you to think about where you would go — into the past or the future. Select a period and a place and when you are ready let your mind move to that time and place. Get out of the machine and continue the fantasy. Where are you ? Notice all the details around you, the landscape, the buildings, if there are any other people etc. Notice yourself and what you are wearing. Who are the other people you are with ? How does it feel ? Just picture that time and place as ideally as you can and picture yourself experiencing life in that time. When you are ready get back in the machine and return to the present.'

Have a discussion about the fantasies. What did you have in your fantasy world that you didn't have here ? In what ways would that fantasy world make you happier ? How could you begin to incorporate some of that fantasy into your present reality ?

PUT YOUR MONEY WHERE YOUR MOUTH IS

A.P.33.

PUT YOUR MONEY WHERE YOUR MOUTH IS

Materials: Pre-printed budget sheets.

Aims: Value systems, self-disclosure and self-awareness.

Procedure: Everyone is allotted one thousand pounds and the money is to be spent on getting what the individual wants or values most. Present the sheets and then allow ten minutes for everyone to work out their own preliminary budget. Acting as an auctioneer, auction off each item and have the group members bid for the items they want. (Items go to the highest bidder.) Group members should make a note of their money spent and the value of each bid, whether or not they got the item, and if they were willing to spend more money than they had originally budgeted.

After the auction have a discussion about the feelings that were generated, e.g. how did you feel when someone else won the item? Was the competition really about the item being auctioned etc.

ATTENDING – NON-ATTENDING

Materials: None.

Aims: Communication, fun.

Procedure: In groups of four, one person is designated as speaker and he/she may talk on any subject for one or two minutes. Two other people are the 'audience': one of them listens attentively and the other doesn't listen. The fourth person is the observer and notes as carefully as possible the behaviours of the other three. Everyone has a go in each of these four roles.

Then discuss what was done in each role. How did you feel in each role? What was seen by the observers? Discuss what you think makes for good attending behaviour.

Variations: Groups of two: one speaker, one attender.
Groups of two: one speaker, one non-attender.
Groups of three: one speaker, one attender, one observer.
Groups of three: one speaker, one non-attender, one observer.

TIME CAPSULE

Materials: Magazines, scissors, glue, tapes and tape recorder.

Aims: Explore values, self-disclosure.

Procedure: Tell the group that they have been chosen to select material to put into a time capsule which will be sealed for two thousand years. They are to select a song title, a photograph and a five minute tape recording.

Discuss: What is expressed by the song title and the photograph ? What are the subject areas of the tape ? What would someone think if they found it in 4000 A.D. ?

FREUD

FREUD

Materials: Slips of paper with families written on. Enough for whole group.

Aims: Improvisation, warm-up, energy release, fun.

Procedure:
(1) Leader prepares family names in groups of four: Papa Freud, Momma Freud, Young Freud, Baby Freud. (Other names: Jung, Perls, Rogers, Klein, Adler etc. Or use animals, fruits etc.)
(2) Slips are passed quickly round the room so that each person has one. Everyone mills around swapping names as they go.
(3) Leader shouts 'Stop'. Everyone immediately starts yelling their family names — Freud, Perls, etc. The family groups gather themselves together and sit down, Papa on the bottom (no matter who has the Papa slip), then Young, then Baby on top.
(4) The last group to be seated in a pile of four loses and has to act out a family scene immediately.
(5) Start over.

FEELING CIRCLE

Materials: None.

Aims: Trust, self-disclosure.

Procedure: Have the group form a circle. Move to the centre and mime an emotion, e.g. anger (growling, yelling, flinging arms), joy/happiness (smiling, laughing, strutting etc). Exaggerate the feeling and go around expressing it to everyone in the circle. Then pick someone to move out to the centre of the circle and mimic your emotion, then both mime the opposite feeling and express this to everyone. Pick someone to continue until everyone has done this.

PEOPLE ROLLING

Materials: None.

Aims: Trust-building, physical activity, fun.

Procedure: Everyone lies face downward in a line. The first person in the line is then rolled over the backs of everyone else and joins the end of the line. The next person is then rolled over the backs, and so on until everyone in the line has rolled and been rolled upon.

MURPHY'S LAW

Materials: Paper and pens or pencils.

Aims: Improvisation, fun, creativity.

Procedure: Divide into small groups of three or four. The leader instructs each group to choose a simple task to enact, e.g. changing a bicycle tyre, and one group enacts their scene. They should enact it accurately.

Members of the other groups write on a piece of paper one way in which the task could go wrong and give the papers to the group who acted the scene.

The group then re-enacts the scene incorporating into it some of the things that can go wrong. Continue with the next group and so on.

Variations: Murphy's corollary: Before you can do one thing you have to do six other things. Just think of all the other things you would have to do before you could change the tyre or whatever and enact them.

SHERLOCK HOLMES (Mark II) *

Materials: Pens and paper may be needed.

Aims: Fun, lateral thinking, deductive reasoning, self-disclosure.

Procedure: Think of an historical figure or a famous or fictional character.
Write down six things that person would have in his/her pocket or purse.
Read out the six things and let the others guess who the person is.

Variations: Choose people known to the group, or choose the teacher or members of the group.
Draw the objects.
Mime the objects.

* For Sherlock Holmes (Mark I) see The Gamesters' Handbook.

SNAKE IN THE GRASS

Materials: None.

Aims: Fun, touch, group awareness.

Procedure: Mark a boundary, the size depending on the number of people playing. One person lies on the ground as the 'snake' and the rest of the players must touch him with one finger. When he calls, 'Snake in the grass', everyone runs, trying not to be tagged by the snake. The snake can only move around on hands and knees to try to catch the other players. The game continues until everyone has been caught. The last player to be caught then becomes the new snake for the next game.

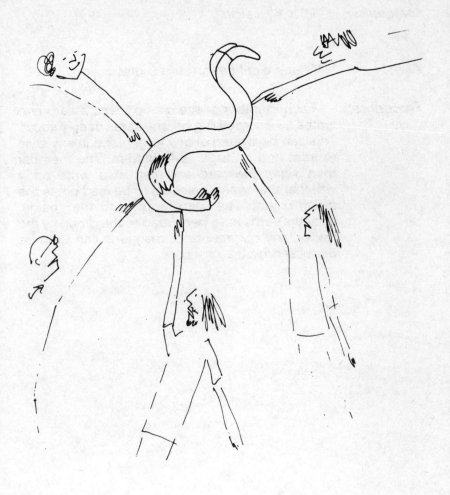

VALUE CARDS

Materials: 4" x 6" cards.

Aims: Values clarification, trust, discussion.

Procedure: Each member of the group takes a card and writes on it something he/she cares deeply about. This can be written at any length and in any style or form and no topic is forbidden. The member then signs the card and can also write on it whether they want their card to be read out to the group or not. The same applies to their name. After the cards have been read to the group by the leader, any comments or reactions can then be discussed by the group.

BLINDMAN'S NUMBERS

Materials: None.

Aims: Sensitivity, trust, fun, group cohesion.

Procedure: The members sit in a group round the room and are numbered. One or more members are chosen to be the blind person and they stand in the centre of the room blindfolded.

The blind person calls out any two numbers and those people stand up and cross the room and the blind person tries to touch them. Anyone who is touched changes places with the blind person.

The game continues and it is important that when the numbers are called out the people stand up immediately and attempt to cross the room.

The players keep the same numbers throughout the game.

KNEE TAPPING

Materials: Chairs or cushions.

Aims: Quick movement, group cohesion, fun.

Procedure: The players sit round in a circle of chairs or cushions and one chair is placed in the centre of the room for the leader. The group leader has a 'tapper' or loosely rolled paper. The leader walks round the circle, taps someone on the knee, goes back to the leader's chair and places the tapper on the chair then goes to the place of the tapped person. It is the aim of the tapped person to try to pick up the tapper and tap the leader with it before the leader reaches his/her chair and sits down. If the tapped person manages to do this the leader is in the circle again. If not there is a new leader and the game continues.

GENERAL POST

Materials: Paper posters.

Aims: Group cohesion, fun.

Procedure: This game is best played with a larger group. Divide the group into two and give each the name of a town, e.g. London, Birmingham, Newcastle, Middlesbrough. Repeat these towns round the circle. The four areas of the room have then been allocated as those towns and a poster is placed on the wall. The members form their own small groups in whichever part of the room their town poster is displayed.

The leader says, 'A letter (or postcard or telegram) is going from ..... to .....' and the players representing the two towns named change places.

If a letter is called, the players walk. If a postcard is called, the players hop.

If a telegram is called, they run.

Variations: Players can sit. The caller stands. The caller has to try and get a chair after the call. One person is left without a chair each time and that person becomes the caller.

THE OLD FAMILY COACH

Materials: None.

Aims: Quick thinking, listening, fun, group cohesion.

Procedure: Everyone sits in a circle with the leader in the middle. The leader makes up a story about 'the old family coach'. Each member is given the name of one of the characters, e.g. father, mother, daughter, son, etc., and the leader begins the story.
When the leader mentions one of the characters the person representing that character stands up, turns round once then sits down again. When the leader mentions the old family coach, all the members of the group stand up, turn round then sit down again.

LOCOMOTION

Materials: Chairs or cushions.

Aims: Movement, fun, group interaction.

Procedure: The players sit in a circle on either cushions or chairs and the leader stands in the middle. The leader then walks or runs round the outside of the circle imitating some means of locomotion, e.g. car, train, rowing, swimming, etc. He stops in front of several people, gives them a signal and they follow him, imitating his form of locomotion. When he has six to ten members behind him he shouts 'All change' and everyone, including the leader, makes for a seat. The one who is left without a seat must re-start with another form of locomotion.

WHO HAS THE BALL ?

Materials: Ball.

Aims: Guessing, fun, group cohesion.

Procedure: The members all sit in a circle on the floor and one player leaves the room. While the player is out of the room the others pass the ball to each other. When the person outside wants to come back he/she must knock three times and enter as quickly as possible after the third knock. The person who is in possession of the ball must hide it somewhere on his/her person and all the other players must look as guilty as possible. It is the aim of the person who has just entered the room to guess who has the ball and where it is hidden.

DEPARTMENT STORE

Materials: Whatever tables, chairs etc. are already in the room.

Aims: Improvisation, drama, fun, characterisation, group interaction.

Procedure: This is what is known as a structured improvisation. (Similar to **The Toyshop** in **The Gamesters' Handbook.**)

(1)   Have group members discuss department stores in general, what they are like, how they operate, what it would be like to be in one late at night after it was locked, how they push products etc. Have them choose whether they want to play the roles of customers, managers, sales people or mannequins. (You might 'brainstorm' all the people you would find in such a store.) Make sure each member knows who he/she is, how old, what they are doing there, which part of the store they would be found in etc. Also what it's like when there is a big sale on.

(2)   'Build' (arrange) the store and have people take their places for the big sale. Do the ritual of opening the doors and letting people in. (Chaos will probably ensue.)

(3)   After a few minutes of letting the scene develop, stop and ask the group how they think

it is going and how they would like to change it. Perhaps they would now like to concentrate on one story line within the scene, or one at a time anyway. It is possible to derive a complete play, even a musical, from this improvisation.

NAME SIX

Materials: None.

Aims: Concentration, quick thinking, fun, creativity, language development.

Procedure: Group members sit in a circle with one who is 'It' in the centre. The person who is 'It' closes his/her eyes.

An object is passed quickly round the circle until 'It' says, 'Stop'.

Whoever has the object is 'It 2'.

'It' gives 'It 2' a letter, such as P.

The object is passed round the circle as quickly as possible and 'It 2' must think of six nouns that begin with P before the object comes back round to him.

If 'It 2' fails to do this, he/she goes into the centre.

Otherwise 'It' stays there and the game starts over.

NAME SIX (Mark II)

Materials: A sign with the list below printed on it.

Aims: Self disclosure, concentration, quick thinking, etc.

Procedure: Same as **Name Six** only instead of naming objects beginning with a certain letter 'It' chooses a subject from the list below and 'It 2' must name six of that subject before the object which is being passed round reaches him/her.

Places you have seen.
Roles you play.
Jobs you have had.
Things you are good at.
Things that embarrass you.
Things you like.
Things you dislike.
Things you hate.

SHOE CARRY RACE

Materials: One shoe for each relay team.

Aims: Fun, physical activity, invention.

Procedure: Line up in relay teams. First person on each team runs down to the end and back, passes the shoe to the next person in the line etc.
The only rule is that the shoe must be carried with a different part of the body each time. This is to be checked on by the referee.

LIAR

Materials: None.

Aims: Group participation, drama, fun.

Procedure: The players are in a circle. One person, A, starts a mime, e.g. lighting a fire.
The person next to him/her says, 'What are you doing?' and A must answer untruthfully, e.g. 'Flying a kite'.
B. then mimes someone flying a kite and when asked 'What are you doing?' must reply with another untruthful answer which the next person has to mime. And so on.
The game continues until everyone in the circle has mimed an action.

MOVE TO THE SPOT

Materials: None.

Aims: Concentration, develop imagination.

Procedure: All group members choose a place in the room as theirs. They walk round the room until the leader says, 'Stop', then they run to their place. Different instructions should be added about how they walk round, e.g.:
Say hello to everyone you pass.
Look down as you walk.
Run round.
Hop round.
Walk backwards.
Bleep as you walk etc.
And about how you get to your spot, e.g.
Directly.
As indirectly as possible.
Slowly.
With your eyes closed etc.

SHOEPILE

Materials: Everyone's shoes.

Aims: Fun, physical activity.

Procedure: Form two teams. All team members take off their shoes and place them in two separate piles. The two piles should be as far apart as possible.

Each team lines up opposite the other team's shoe pile.

Each team has to crawl across the room to the other team's shoe pile and they have two minutes to tie all the laces together or hide the shoes within boundaries, (or both), then crawl back.

After two minutes at a signal everyone runs to find their shoes and the first team with all their shoes on, laces tied, and sitting down, wins.

Variations: Do the whole game, or any part of it, with eyes closed.

SHOE CIRCLE

Materials: One shoe.

Aims: Fun, physical activity, touching.

Procedure: Group stand in a circle and pass the shoe round without using their hands or dropping it. Time the pass and try again if you want to.
OR
Have four goes round the circle, once with chins, once with feet, once with knees, once with elbows.

SHOELACE RELAY

Materials: One lace-up shoe per team.

Aims: Fun, physical activity.

Procedure: Line up in teams. First person runs down to the end with shoe in hand and lace in the other, sits down, laces shoe, runs back and hands it to the next person who must run down, unlace it, run back etc. Team sitting down first at the end wins.

WALTER'S TOES

Materials: Everyone's toes.

Aims: Fun, touch, laughter.

Procedure: Find a partner and decide who is A and who is B.
Decide between you one noise that you can use to signal 'hot' and another noise to signal 'cold'. A lies down and secretly chooses a place on his/her body to be 'the spot'. B searches for 'the spot' by probing gently with his/her toes. A makes 'hot' and 'cold' noises.
When the spot is found, A shouts 'Bonanza' or 'Eureka' or something, and they then change places and sounds for the next round.

CHEQUERBOARD

Materials: Copy of **The Rubaiyat of Omar Khayam.**

Aims: Lead into Drama, explore issues about destiny, free will etc.

Procedure: Read, or, preferably, display the lines from the poem:

'Tis all a chequerboard of nights and days
Where Destiny with men for pieces plays
Hither and thither moves, and mates, and slays,
And one by one back in the closet lays.'

Have someone play the role of Destiny, and find a way to have Destiny move the pieces, controlling their lives and actions. This can be done to music non-verbally, or it can be done in small groups with dialogue. It can be explored in many different ways and can be made into a production piece if desired. A discussion about the concept of our lives being controlled by Destiny can be very stimulating. What happens when people protest against the fate that has been dealt them?

Variations: Do the same with other poems, such as **Jaberwocky** (mysteriously or comically), **The King's Breakfast** (explore sexist issues) etc.

Use a chess game or a chequers game or **Monopoly, Pit,** or any other board game.

N.B. I first experienced being a piece on the Chequerboard when I was studying with Dorothy Heathcote, so I owe this idea — to name but one — to her.

CROSSED AND UNCROSSED

Materials: A pair of scissors.

Aims: Fun, observation, lateral thinking.

Procedure: A pair of scissors is passed round the circle. The person passing the scissors says, 'I pass these scissors crossed' or 'I pass these scissors uncrossed.' Each time they are passed the leader agrees or disagrees with the statement. No indication is given as to what 'crossed' and 'uncrossed' refers to. Group members have to guess and check out their guess by joining the leader's agree/disagree comments when they think they know the meaning. The game should continue until nearly all the group are correctly calling 'agree/disagree' and saying 'crossed' or 'uncrossed'.

N.B. 'Crossed' and 'uncrossed' actually refers to the passer's legs. It does not matter whether the scissors are crossed or not.

MISTER MEN

Materials: Wall chart of **Mister Men.**

Aims: To get children (and adults!) to understand about adverbs and adjectives.

Procedure: One person goes out of the room and the rest of the group choose one of the **Mister Men.** When the person comes back he/she says, 'Who has just visited you?' The rest of the group says, 'We can't tell you.' The person who was sent out then asks individual members of the group how he walked in, how he drinks his tea, how he sits down etc., until the correct **Mister Man** is guessed.

TAG VARIATIONS

Materials: None.

Aims: Ice-breaker, involvement.

Procedure:

A.   Cat and Mouse Tag.

The group stand in pairs one behind the other and spread around the room. Two people — cat and mouse — chase each other around all the pairs. Mouse can take refuge by jumping on the back of a member of the group. This person then becomes the mouse. If cat catches mouse they continue with the roles reversed.

In a large group more than one cat and mouse pair can operate at one time.

B.   Dragon Tail.

The dragon chases all other group members. When someone is caught, he/she holds on to the dragon by the waist and they then continue the chase. The game continues until all except one are part of the dragon.

Variation :   Dragon's Tail (Game No. I.15)

C. Chain Tag.

The group members caught form a chain by holding hands.

D. Release Tag.

When caught, each group member stands on the spot with legs apart. Other group members can release a caught person by crawling through their legs.

E. Tag and hold it.

When caught, the person must hold the part of the body that was tagged. In this way, obstacles are formed by caught group members.

F. Blind tag.

Everyone is in pairs. One pair are 'it'. They try to tag all the other pairs. One member of each pair, (including the 'it' pair) is blindfolded.

INTRODUCTORY GAMES

CONTENTS

I.1.	Human treasure hunt	Page 97
I.2.	Opening rounds	Page 99
I.3.	Fingertips	Page 100
I.4.	Bumpety bumpety bump	Page 101
I.5.	Celebrities	Page 102
I.6.	Autobiographies	Page 103
I.7.	George's name game	Page 104
I.8.	Categories	Page 105
I.9.	Play with your name	Page 106
I.10.	Find your partner	Page 107
I.11.	Absent friends I and II	Page 108
	Absent friends III	Page 110
I.12.	Pig, wolf and farmer	Page 111
I.13.	Things I do badly	Page 112
I.14.	Octopus	Page 113
I.15.	Dragon's tail	Page 114
I.16.	Indian poker	Page 116
I.17.	Allies	Page 118
I.18.	Shoozy doozy name game	Page 119
I.19.	What am I doing here ?	Page 120
I.20.	Catch my name	Page 121

HUMAN TREASURE HUNT

Materials: Treasure hunt list or chart.

Aims: Breaking the ice.

Procedure: Follow the directions below not necessarily in order, approaching mostly people you did not know before. Briefly record their responses. Stay with your partner until the instruction is given to move on.

1. Find someone who has recently been on a long trip. Ask them to tell you about it.
2. Find someone who has socks like yours and discuss the subject of socks with them.
3. Find a person with whom you think you might have a lot in common and talk to them to see if that is true.
4. Find someone with a nose like yours and have a dialogue about noses.
5. Find someone who has your birth sign and talk about astrological personality characteristics.
6. Interview someone who wears glasses. Find out how it affects their life.
7. Find someone you wouldn't mind being stuck in a lift with. Discuss claustrophobia.
8. Move around the room saying a line from your favourite poem, song or film until you find

someone who knows the next line. Discuss the poem, song, film with them.

9. Find someone in the room whom you think has a dark secret. Try to convince them to tell you what it is.

10. Decide who is your favourite composer or musician. Try to find someone in the room who shares that view. If you can't, try to convince someone that he/she ought to share it.

N.B.   Instead of having a chart or list; the facilitator just calls out one instruction at a time.

OPENING ROUNDS

Materials: None.

Aims: Breaking the ice.

Procedure: Do a round of:

The best thing that happened to me this week,
If I were an animal I'd be a ....(because ....)
If I were a piece of fruit (or a song, or a dance, or a famous person) I'd be .....
I'd like to write a book about ....
Some things I want to do before I die are .....
I did my homework and this is what happened ....
I didn't do my homework and this is what happened ....
If I had last week to live over what I would change is ....
Mime or sculpt how you are feeling now.
State how you are feeling at the moment.

OR

Do two rounds of:

1. What do I want from this group ?
2. What do I really, really want from this group ?

I.3.

FINGERTIPS

Materials: None.

Aims: Warm-up, fun, relaxation, trust-building.

Procedure: Group members stand in a circle at arms'
length with their eyes closed. They raise their
arms and touch finger tips. The leader says, 'Be
aware of the touch of your fingertips, follow any
movement that comes up in you, let it take you.
Don't lead, just follow.' The leader lets the group
move where the impulse takes it until he/she
chooses to end it with the instruction, 'Freeze'.
The leader then says, 'Open your eyes and be
aware of where you are.'

Variations: Play outdoors.
Use blindfolds.
Start from different positions, e.g. lying down.

BUMPETY BUMP BUMP

Materials: None.

Aims: Ice-breaking, fun, concentration, learning names, mixing.

Procedure: The group forms a circle with one person in the centre. The people in the circle must find out the names of the people on their left and right. The person in the centre points at someone and says EITHER 'Left bumpety bump bump' OR 'Right bumpety bump bump.' The person pointed at must respond with the first name of the person next to him/her on the right or left, according to the instruction given. If he/she does not say the name before the person in the middle has said the final 'bump' he/she is in the middle. The game should be played fast.

Variations: Have more than one person in the centre. Use capital cities, colours etc. instead of names.

I.5.

CELEBRITIES

Materials: None.

Aims: Introduction, warm-up, communication, fun.

Procedure: People mill around the room stopping in front of a partner when the leader tells them to. The leader gives a starting sentence, e.g. 'When I saw you on the telly last night . . . ' The first partner has to start with that sentence and carry on, somehow relating it to the other person, e.g. 'When I saw you on the telly last night I couldn't help noticing your charming smile and the way your eyes sparkled.' The leader then gives the second partner a new sentence, e.g. 'When I saw you at the ambassador's party I thought . . . '

Other examples:
My mother always used to warn me about people like you . . .
Having found myself in this position, I must just say . . .
I know you're a judge but . . .
Now listen, dear, I just want to tell you . . . etc.

I.6.

AUTOBIOGRAPHIES

Materials: None.

Aims: Warm-up, getting to know people, self-awareness, self-disclosure, fun, memory.

Procedure: Get a partner, preferably one you don't know. Decide which one is A and which one B. A has three minutes (longer if you like) to tell B about his/her life, starting as far back as possible and continuing in chronological order. B just listens. At the end of three minutes they change round and B talks. At the end of the second three minutes the leader tells them to change partners and decide which is A and B. A carries on from where he/she left off without filling in the missing information and takes three minutes as before. Then it is his new partner's turn. This whole process is repeated three times in this manner and then on the fourth round the leader instructs the partners to talk about their auto-biography of the future.

Variations: Played the same way but with reference to a specific aspect of life, e.g. jobs, dreams, friend-ships etc.

GEORGE'S NAME GAME

Materials: Large sheet or blanket.

Aims: Ice-breaking, fun, concentration, learning names.

Procedure: Two people hold the blanket and the rest of the group divide into two equal groups one at either side of the blanket. An appointed member of each group goes up to the blanket and when it is dropped the first one to say the other person's name wins.

Variations: Depending upon which materials are available for screening, the screen could be lifted, moved from side to side or dropped.

CATEGORIES

Materials: None.

Aims: Ice breaker, fun, identification, release of tension, self-awareness, values clarification.

Procedure: All sit in a circle, the leader calls out the names of groups of people, e.g. dog lovers, spectacle wearers, smokers, members of sports teams etc. The people who belong to such groups get up and go into the middle and when another category is called people either stay where they are and others join them or sit down if they do not belong to that newly called group. This can be continued at a fast pace to get people moving.

Variations: Leadership can change to anyone calling out categories.
'Brainstorm' categories.

PLAY WITH YOUR NAME

Materials:　　None.

Aims:　　Release energy, name game, personal statement, release inhibitions.

Procedure:　　Beginning in a circle, one person can go into the middle of the room and do some kind of action which reflects the way they are feeling at the moment. At the same time they say their name. Everyone has to do exactly the same thing moving about the room. When the first person is ready to stop he/she can tap someone else on the shoulder and that person then starts a new type of movement.

Variations:　　Anyone can take over by calling their own name and instigating a new action.

FIND YOUR PARTNER

Materials: Paper, pencils or cards.

Aims: Ice breaker, group interaction, fun, forming pairs for another game.

Procedure: Everyone stands in a circle and the leader gives each person a piece of paper with the name of an animal written on it. Everyone then goes round making the noise of that animal until they find the second person who is also making that animal sound.
When everyone has found their partner, further categories can be given, e.g. look for all four-legged animal groups, those found in farmyards etc.

Variations: The game can be mimed using the names of famous people, nursery rhymes etc. According to the number of members in the group the game can be extended from two's to four's, eight's and so on.

ABSENT FRIENDS I

Materials: None.

Aims: Time utilisation (waiting for the whole group to arrive), fun, imagination.

Procedure: The first members to arrive sit in a circle and in a round they answer the question, 'Who is the next person you would like to see coming through the door and what would you like to say to them?' The wished-for arrival could be someone you know and love, someone you would like to tell off, someone who is dead or far away whom you would like to see again, a celebrity, a fictional character etc.

Variations: In turns, when the group member arrives you greet him/her as your answer was and say exactly what you wanted to say.

ABSENT FRIENDS II

Procedure: Invent a story to explain the absence of each missing member of the group. This can be done with a round, each person adding a new sentence or paragraph to the story, or it can be done as an individual narrative or a role play.

ABSENT FRIENDS

ABSENT FRIENDS III

Procedure: Do a round of 'People I never want to see again.' Describe the person and say what has happened to make you not want to see him/her again. Imagine what you would like to do or say if you did meet that person.

Variations: Role play the meetings.

I.12.

PIG, WOLF AND FARMER

Materials: None.

Aims: Fun, team game, strategy, group interaction.

Procedure: The group splits into two teams which face each other. There are three choices — pig, wolf or farmer, and the leader explains that pig takes wolf, wolf takes farmer, and farmer takes pig. Each group then decides which one of the three they wish to be and when they have decided they face the other team again. There are three different signs for the three; pig, wiggle both index fingers either side of your head; wolf, hold out your sharp claws; farmer, a digging action. At the count of three, both teams move towards each other and then display their action to the other team. There is a points system and whichever team 'takes' the other, (as described above) wins a point.

Variations: Each team works out five 'plays' in advance. Take one person from the other side each time you win.
Three teams and three different ways of gaining points.

THINGS I DO BADLY

Materials: None.

Aims: Self-disclosure, self-awareness, trust building, group cohesion.

Procedure: (1) In a round each person has a turn at saying the thing they do most badly e.g. 'I am very bad at keeping my accounts straight.'
(2) The next round everyone says the thing people tell them they do well, e.g. 'People say I'm a very good cook.'
(3) The next round everyone says the thing they know they do well, e.g. 'I am very good at keeping my house tidy.'
(4) The leader asks everyone to exaggerate the thing they do well and everyone stands, mills around and when they meet someone they 'brag' about the thing they do well, e.g. 'I'm the world champion at . . .)
(5) Follow with either a discussion of the exercise or a round saying how it felt.

N.B. The leader should take the first turn in each round, setting an example of making the statement and then elaborating it for two or three sentences.

OCTOPUS

Materials: Two boundary markers.

Aims: Fun, physical activity.

Procedure: Mark two boundary lines, Players are safe behind these. One person stands in the centre and shouts 'Go'. The object is to cross to the other line without being caught. The 'octopus' in the centre has a ball which he/she throws to catch people. If you are touched you must freeze on the spot and become part of the octopus. You are allowed to use your arms as tentacles to catch people as they run past. Everyone who is touched must freeze on the spot and become a tentacle.

The game continues until all the players have been turned into tentacles either by being touched by other players or hit by the ball.

The last person to be caught starts off the next game as the octopus by shouting 'Go' and throwing the ball to catch people.

DRAGON'S TAIL

Materials: Brightly coloured scarf or handkerchief.

Aims: Physical activity, fun.

Procedure: Two dragons are formed by people holding on to one another's waists in a long line. The last person in the line has a brightly coloured handkerchief tucked into his/her trousers or belt. (This is the dragon's tail). The object is to catch the tail of the other dragon without losing your own tail in the process.

Variations: More than two dragons.
One dragon and try to catch your own tail.

115

INDIAN POKER

Materials: Pairs of cards with slogans. Pins or tapes to attach them.

Aims: Fun, mixing, improvisation, empathy, creativity.

Procedure:
1.   Divide the group into two teams and separate the teams from each other.
2.   Take one card from each matching pair for each team so that one person on each team has the same card as a person on the other team.
3.   Tape the card on each person's forehead or pin it at the neck of a shirt or blouse so that people cannot read their own cards.
4.   Team A members will mill around at one end of the room; Team B at the other end (or in separate rooms) and they read each other's cards, reacting subtly to what the cards say. No one must read a card aloud or tell people what is on their own cards.
5.   After a few minutes of this — after each team has had plenty of time to read and react to all the cards — join the two teams together with the instruction, 'Find the person who has the same card as you

do. When you have found that person, take their hand and sit down with them. Share how it felt having that card.'

Ideas for cards:

1. As you look at me you can't help noticing that I'm turning into a werewolf.
2. I talk too much. Get me to listen.
3. Treat me as if I were friendly but not very bright.
4. I'm lonely. Help me to meet other people.
5. Find out about my family without asking directly.
6. Behave as if I were six years old.
7. Mirror my gestures and face while we are talking.
8. I'm very popular. Try to become my friend.
9. I feel warm and loving. Hug me.
10. Disapprove of everything I say.
11. I make you nervous. Show me how nervous you are.
12. Look over my right shoulder when you talk to me etc.

ALLIES

Materials: None.

Aims: Ice breaker, self-disclosure, fun, trust. (To be played at the beginning of a group or course.)

Procedure: (1) Group members all mill around. Leader says, 'Find someone you don't know who has the same expectations as you do about this course.'
(2) Leader says, 'Sit down with the person you've found and decide which of you is A and which is B.
(3) A talks first. B just listens. A talks about 'some things I want you to know about me.' After five minutes they change over and B talks while A listens for another five minutes.
(4) Leader says, 'Now have a chat.' Agree on some things that the two of you have in common. (Five more minutes.)
(5) Leader now says, 'Find and interview another couple. Keep going until you find some 'allies' who agree with you about some things. Now form two larger alliances until the group is in two teams.'
(6) Play a game such as **Pig, Wolf and Farmer** or **Human noughts and crosses** or else do a value continuum in each team.

Variations: Keep going with number five until the whole group is together and has agreed about something.

SHOOZY DOOZY NAME GAME

Materials: One shoe.

Aims: Ice breaker, learn names, fun, activity.

Procedure: 1. Group sits in a circle with 'it' in the centre.
2. 'It' introduces him/her self to the group, throws the shoe up (not too hard !) and yells out a description of any two people in the group, e.g. 'The girl in the red jumper and the man in the green shoes'.
3. Both people described run for the centre and try to grab the shoe. The one that gets it is 'it' and has to introduce him/her self, the other person called, and the previous 'it' to the group.

WHAT AM I DOING HERE ?

Materials: Blank cards (2" x 4"), blackboard and chalk.

Aims: Group introduction, individual aims, group cohesion, commitment, fun.

Procedure: (1) 'Brainstorm' all possible aims for being in the group. Someone charts these on the board.
(2) Each reason is then copied on to two cards.
(3) Cards are shuffled and six cards are dealt to each player.
(4) Players then trade cards with the intention of ending up with their top three aims.
(5) After trading, players sit in a circle and say which three cards they have and whether they own their three cards.
(6) As the players share their cards someone checks against the original 'brainstorm' list and marks off the number of times the same reason is given, and adds new ones.

Variations: Ask the players what they want to get out of the course rather than their reasons for being there.

CATCH MY NAME

Materials: None.

Aims: Introductory, warm-up.

Procedure: After a round in which people say their names, a member of the group is given a ball. He/she throws it to someone. The catcher has to call out the name of the thrower and then throw the ball to another group member who then calls out the name of the new thrower, and so on. All the group members' names therefore become familiar. Stop the game when all the names are known to all members.

GROUP LEADERS' GAMES

CONTENTS

G.L.1.	Chairs Game	Page 127
G.L.2.	Johari's Window	Page 128
G.L.3.	Sabotage (Mark II)	Page 130
G.L.4.	Group Sculpture	Page 131
G.L.5.	Endgame I	Page 132
	Endgame II	Page 132
	Endgame III	Page 133
G.L.6.	Anarchy	Page 134
G.L.7.	Deformities	Page 135

CHAIRS GAME

Materials:　　Two chairs or cushions.

Aims:　　Self-awareness.

Procedure:　　The leader asks for volunteers and waits till they come forward. Then the leader asks the volunteers to share with the rest of the group what went on in their heads between the voice that said you should volunteer and the voice that said you shouldn't.

Two chairs or cushions are used to denote the two voices and the leader asks the first person various questions. The person moves towards whichever chair is applicable.

Suggested questions are:

Which voice seemed stronger ?

Which voice usually wins ?

Could you label the two voices, e.g.

'bossy', 'cautious', 'scared' etc. ?

JOHARI'S WINDOW

Materials: Pencil, paper, model of Johari's window:

Things that others know (about me) e.g. my name, what my face looks like etc.	Things others know and I don't (about me) e.g. what my back looks like as I walk
Things I know others don't know (about me) e.g. my secret wish	Things no one knows (about me) e.g. my life ten years from now.

Aims: Self-awareness, self-disclosure, sharing.

Procedure: All group members draw their own Johari's window, filling in several examples in each separate pane.
Leader helps the group discuss and share some of their examples.
Group then chooses which pane they want to explore. This can be done through art, drama, sharing in pairs, sharing in the circle etc.

Pane 3 is good for getting feedback from other people about how we sound, what impressions we make etc.

N.B. This is a classic game — so much so that I no longer remember where I first saw it. I am grateful to the inventors who — far from being a pair of mystical Indian gurus, were rumoured to have been two guys named Joe and Harry.

SABOTAGE (Mark II)

Materials: Cards which have on them the letters A,B,C and D.

Aims: To make people conscious of how they sabotage themselves and their relationships. Fun, assertiveness training, communication.

Procedure: (1)   Pass out cards and form small groups each group to contain an A,B,C and D.
(2)   C and D decide together a way in which they can form a collusive partnership in relation to which A should have a legitimate role, e.g. C is mother, D is daughter, A is father who is being excluded.
(3)   While C and D meet, A talks to B about the kind of support he likes to have in his life situation.
(4)   C and D inform A of the situation and begin a role play.
(5)   A's task is to become assertive in becoming included in the relations between C and D.
(6)   C and D's tasks are to maintain their relationship and sabotage A's inclusion.
(7)   B's role is to support A and to make positive suggestions.

Variations: After the exercise discuss the outcomes in small groups.
Switch roles and start again.

GROUP SCULPTURE

Materials: None.

Aims: Self-expression, self-image, group image.

Procedure: One member of the group makes a sculpture by using all the other group members. They can be put in any position in relation to each other. The sculptor can include him/herself. (This is useful in a fairly small group.) Time should be given for each group member to move outside the sculpture and look at it.

Variations: Group members can spontaneously change their positions when the sculptor has finished. The group can express their feelings about their positions in the sculpture. Noises can be added.

ENDGAME I

Materials: One ball of string.

Aims: Saying goodbye, getting closure at the end of a group.

Procedure: Sit in a circle. One person holds the ball of string, looks around and says a goodbye and a final message to someone else, tossing the ball of string but holding on to the end of it.

The person who receives the message and string then repeats the process. This can continue as long as it seems productive and interesting.

At the end there is silence and someone cuts all the strings that are now criss-crossing the circle, thus symbolising the end of the group.

ENDGAME II

Sit in a circle, clear up any unfinished business. One person leaves as if to go home. Outside the room that person thinks about what else he/she would like to say and the people in the group also think of any messages they would like to give that person. The person returns to the room and gives and receives all the messages. The process is repeated with as many people as want a turn. The leader must facilitate the whole thing from getting ponderous or sloppy.

ENDGAME III

Devise a throne or raised dais of cushions etc. Each person takes a turn to sit on the throne and share his/her feelings about the group.

ANARCHY

Materials:　　None.

Aims:　　Creativity, confusion, laughter, freedom to explore.

Procedure:　　Divide into groups of three or four and tell the groups to 'invent a game with no rules'.
Do not give any other instructions except to encourage them to play their game rather than talk about it.
Watch what happens and accept that some people may get quite upset.
Allow time for de-briefing and feedback.

CONCLUSION

The bell rang, the door opened, the teacher stood aside, and we moved into the empty classroom . . . . It was empty! My first day of school, and not a picture, not a chair, not a desk, *empty!* I couldn't believe it. We must have come to the wrong place.

But my mother was still leading me forward, looking quite unsurprised. I sat on the floor in a corner of the room with the other children, and the teacher sat down among us.

She smiled at us and said, 'I imagine you're wondering why this doesn't look like a classroom to you. The reason it is this way is that it's your room, and you can choose how you want it to be. I will help you to make it any way you want it.'

SILENCE

'You can tell me your ideas, all of them, and then we'll choose.'

SILENCE

The ideas began to come slowly at first. And six weeks later we had built a town, a functioning village, in the empty room. We had a bakery with all shapes of cookies, a pet shop with at least three guinea pigs, six white mice and some baby chicks, and an assorted rotating population of our own pets. We had a bank with real money, and a doctor's office next to the chemist's, which had a supply of antiseptics and plasters. The shops were built like carnival booths and we had built them ourselves; perhaps the walls and shelves were crooked, perhaps our imaginations had to fill in the gaps in the merchandise, my memory of it is that it was perfect, and we had built it, and we lived in it and played in it and worked in it.

Need I say that, in order to build it, we had been learning words to write on signs, and writing them, and measuring wood, and hammering nails, and adding sums, and baking bread and cookies. And lots more.

The concept of starting from nothingness and moving through curiosity towards discovery, creativity, purposeful-as-opposed-to-

137

rote learning, accruing knowledge and skills along the way, is not a new one (the incident described took place forty-two years ago), and glorious lip service has been paid to it in the intervening decades. Perhaps drama teachers have been the most instrumental in advancing these kinds of teaching methods, the ones that are aimed at discovery, self-knowledge and improved self-concept. I have been in contact with hundreds of teachers in California and in England, and I don't know many who are willing to abdicate the position of being in possession of the key to learning and knowledge, so that the learners can discover the key themselves.

The memory of that empty classroom, and others like it, shaped the kind of teacher I became twenty years later. Over the eighteen years that I worked as a classroom teacher, drama specialist, Gestalt therapist and group leader, and then as a lecturer, I found myself increasingly able to be a facilitator of learning by emptying my mind and the environment of preconceived ideas and plans. It was a very liberating feeling to shed the responsibility of all knowledge, wisdom, choice, assessment, passing of exams, and turn it over to the learners so that we could participate in the process together.

Among the tools which I developed during those years one of the most delightful, powerful, and effective was the use of games. Although some of the games were with me from my own childhood, and some from my training as a group leader and drama teacher, most of them I accumulated, invented, gleaned from the children, students and other teachers. I learned how to use them purposefully to enhance the learning process and improve our communication with each other, our knowledge of ourselves and our enjoyment of school. I used to carry the games and ideas around with me on bits of envelopes and old shopping lists, in a plastic bag.

Then I found myself in the Teaching Training Game at Bede College in Durham, lecturing about humanistic methods of teaching and spending a lot of time sitting in my office explaining the same games and ideas to dozens of individual students about to go on teaching practice. And so, out of need, and finally laziness, **Gamesters' Handbook** was born and my ideas were compiled along with those of my friend and fellow drama teacher, Howard Phillips. In our impatience to have the book in our hands and on our shelves, we published it ourselves before giving it to Hutchinson, and it began to be ordered from all over the world by group leaders, scout leaders, social workers, prison officers, group workers of all sorts, and, most of all, by drama teachers.

People have said to me, 'Isn't there a danger of people using the book without knowing how?' And others: 'Perhaps the book should be banned from the classroom unless the teacher demonstrates that she knows how to use it.' My answer to that (apart from the fact that I am violently allergic to sentences which begin, 'Isn't there a danger of . . . ?' Yes, there's danger; life is dangerous unless you want to be a hermit or live your life in a padded cell, and growth comes from taking risks) is that the games can be played on a very simple level, just for fun, or on a continuum of more advanced levels, stretched, expanded, integrated into school curriculum, drama, counselling and group work. The beauty of the games we are discussing is that they are so highly adaptable and that they are non-competitive for the most part. As a self-styled 'expert' I have played the games with every possible kind of group including blind people, handicapped, elderly and mentally disturbed people, infants, students, social workers, teachers, doctors and nurses, and some of my best friends. I have played them on the floor, in chairs, at desks, in the car, on airplanes, on a boat and in the desert. And one of the outcomes of all this experience is that I am firmly convinced that *anyone* can use the games constructively, even at the most matter-of-fact level, and that people can be quite easily trained to expand upon them and upon their uses.

Let's look at one of the more popular games, **Fear in a hat**, and take it through various levels of use.

Materials	Pencil, paper, 'hat' or tin etc.
Aims	Share and accept.
Procedure	Played in a circle. Ask everyone, including leader, to complete this sentence, (anonymously); 'In this class

(or group or whatever) I am afraid that . . .' Put the scraps of paper in the tin or receptacle in the centre. Pass the tin round. Each person has to draw a sentence out and read it, enlarging on the sentence and trying to express what the person was feeling. For example, the leader reads the first one and might say, 'In this class I am afraid I will be laughed at . . . (continues talking) I am afraid to say my feelings because everyone laughs at me, so I never say anything.' Continue round the circle. Leader must make sure that everyone just listens and does not comment. No arguing or comment is allowed. Then discuss what was noticed or discovered.

Variations   Likes and dislikes in a hat (two tins).
Worries in a hat.
Gripes in a hat.
Wishes in a hat, etc.

As pointed out in the instructions the sentences could be about any subject, such as wishes, hopes etc., but let us suppose that they actually were about fear in this case.

After the first round of the game as described above one could start a discussion in the group, or do any number of follow-up activities including:

1   In pairs, talk about times in your life when you have been afraid of that particular thing, and when you have felt the other person's fear.

2   In pairs, talk about what's the worst thing that could happen. For example, if your fear was fear of the dark, talk about what might happen in the dark, what might be lurking there, what if you were blind etc.

3   In pairs or in the group, discuss whether or not you shared the same fears as other people. How do you avoid/face/cope with those fears?

4 Close your eyes and have a fantasy about a very extreme situation in which you are faced with your particular fear. Then discuss: Can you really feel that fear now, can you induce it in your fantasy? How do you know when you are afraid? What bodily changes do you go through? Which comes first, the fear as an awareness in your mind, or the bodily changes?

5 Draw:
A   fantasy scene of your fear.
B   monsters in shape of your own fears.
C   make masks of your fears and wear them and be them.

6 Either in discussion or on paper or through drama relate fear to your senses. How does your fear
> feel
> taste
> smell
> look
> sound?

7 Using any of the above media, explore the differences between fear and any other strong emotion negative or positive. What are the different bodily reactions, how do other people relate to you at those times etc.

8 Fantasize about your own fear. Move around the room making your face and body reflect extreme fear in that situation. Add noises.

9 Brainstorm together:
A   things I'm afraid of.
B   people I'm afraid of.
C   situations I'm afraid of.
Write, draw, dramatise, make music about these.

10 Do a Value Continuum[1] about fear, using such extremes as, 'I am never afraid .... I am often afraid', or 'It's all right to be afraid sometimes .... it's never all right to be afraid.'

11 'Psychodrama': the group takes someone's fear to act out as a

scene, adds details, sound, action. The 'client' can choose to direct it or star in it. It can be repeated several times with different endings so that the client has an opportunity to see what works and what doesn't.

12 The group invents games and ideas and plays to explore the subject of fear. In my opinion, the most fruitful of all.

13 There is the possibility, with a trained leader, of using this game as a basis for 'working' on a specific aspect of a client's fears, using Gestalt, transactional analysis, counselling, or in-depth psychodrama.

I want to re-emphasise that although I have fun with these games, socially and professionally, that is not my sole purpose in playing them, nor is it all that they achieve; I take them very seriously as a powerful and valuable group work tool.

Here are a few examples of the rewards I get from using the games purposefully as a teacher or group leader:

A I have proved to myself over and over that if I spend a few hours or even days using these activities with each group of pupils/students at the beginning of a new term, I will have fewer discipline problems, better communication and rapport, a more open and supportive group, and more co-operation for whatever tasks we have to accomplish together.

B These activities encourage me to listen to the students and be receptive to their ideas and to get to know them better.

C The games promote creativity and lateral thinking and can be adapted for any subject. (The first games I used in schools were Maths games; try applying **The rule of the game** to Maths, Science, Politics, etc.)

D 'Rounds'² create an opportunity for each member of a group to be heard without comment or evaluation. For some quiet students this may be the only such opportunity.

E The rounds foster a spirit of equality rather than hierarchy or competition.

142

F Rounds proved a valuable source of feedback for me as a teacher, and for the methods of learning.

G These activities have proved extremely valuable in the exploration teacher and enhancement of self image.[3]

Obviously these are the kinds of things that teachers accomplish using many different methods, notably drama. I know that the games are not a panacea and not the only means to these ends. And they have been so effective and valuable for me as a teacher that I am willing to do whatever I can to encourage their use.

For those of you who have not tried games and other discovery methods in your teaching, here are thirteen ready-made reasons why 'It won't work in school':

1 The Head won't let me.
2 The other teachers will think I'm just playing around.
3 It would make too much noise.
4 I don't have a place to do it in.
5 There's no time because of exams.
6 Isn't there a danger of ... (whatever you care to name).
7 People won't talk honestly in the classroom.
8 They'll make a joke of it.
9 What if they get upset?
10 It doesn't go with my subject.
11 The Deputy head won't let me.
12 The parents wouldn't like it.
13 I don't know how.
14
15
16
17
18
19
20
    (Add seven more of your own)

I'd like to ask you to take a look at the possibility that these are just considerations that you are using to stop yourself trying new things. Try to make a list of thirteen reasons why your school or group could benefit from exploring these ideas, or thirteen ways round your considerations. And try something – anything – new in your work tomorrow.

Donna Brandes 198

References

1 **Values clarification**, Sidney Simon. Also appears in **Gamesters Handbook**, Donna Brandes and Howard Phillips, (Stanle Thornes, 1978.)
2 See 'Basic strategies' page 8, **Gamesters' Handbook**.
3 See **The Hope Street Experience** by Donna Brandes. (Acces Publishing, Leeds, 1981)

This conclusion was written with the help of Diana Howard an Tom Herron and the co-author of **Gamesters' Handbook**, Howar Phillips, and first appeared in **The London Drama Magazine** und the title **How Games Grew**.